CW00889205

ANGER MANAGEMENT:

A Guide on How to Control Your Life and Deal with Your Relationships

By Alan Tucker

Copyright 2015 - All Rights Reserved –
Alan Tucker

ALL RIGHTS RESERVED. No part of
this publication may be reproduced or
transmitted in any form whatsoever,
electronic, or mechanical, including
photocopying, recording, or by any
informational storage or retrieval system
without express written, dated and
signed permission from the author.

Amazon Offers on Best-Selling Books

I want to reward you for starting to read my book. We both know that wisdom comes from books.

I'm working with a bunch of awesome people and, from time to time, I publish my books on their site, either for a huge discount or absolutely free.

If you love reading as much as I do, register using your e-mail address here: http://bit.ly/1M7CVVC

Table of Contents

Chapter 1:

Understanding Anger

What is anger?

Anger is just one of the many emotions that we experience in our daily lives. The intensity of anger can range from mild irritation all the way up to rage. Anger kicks in as our body's response to a threat. It could be a threat to ourselves, or a threat to someone or something that we love.

Anger is a complex emotion; it is made up of three components:

1. The physical reactions. These include an elevated heart rate, high blood pressure, and tense muscles.
2. The cognitive experience. These are the thoughts that go through our head when we are angry, and how we think about the situation that lead to it. For example, our

thoughts may tell us that we have been treated unfairly.
3. How we express anger. The behavioural signals for anger include turning red, raising our voice, slamming doors, or storming off. As individuals we each express our anger in different ways. One person might express their anger by shouting, while another might express theirs by giving the silent treatment. How we express our anger is very much dependant on our personality type.

Is Anger Normal?

Anger, just like every human emotion, is completely normal. Not expressing anger is in fact unhealthy, as it is an indicator that you are stifling your emotions instead of expressing them. When expressed in a healthy way, anger can be a productive emotion. It is only when anger begins to interfere with your daily life, health, and happiness that is becomes problematic.

What Happens Inside your Brain when you get Angry?

Anger comes from primal instinct. It is hard-wired into our brains through the process of evolution. However, some aspects of the emotion are also societal. Over the years, society has become much more accepting of hostile displays of anger or frustration. When you get angry, a lot goes on inside your brain.

Some scientists believe that anger developed in order to help our species survive. Anger most likely aided our ancestors by helping them fight for scarce resources, which in turn helped them prevail in the natural selection race.

Anger is triggered in a part of our brain known as the amygdala. It is a very primitive part of the brain. It's the area where you first start to get worked up when something makes you angry. It is like the alarm that causes the other parts of your body to react to the anger. Next, your adrenal glands will kick into action by pumping adrenaline and creating an adrenaline rush in the body. This causes your heart rate to increase, which can cause a fluttering sensation in your chest. Some people can also become aggressive at this point due to an increase in testosterone in the body.

Now that your body is beginning to show the physical signs of anger, our brains are also kicking into rage mode. You will begin to talk faster and louder. Your facial muscles send a warning to the people around you as they twitch, causing a scowl to creep across your face.

Our brains also have the ability to pick up on small clues indicating that someone is angry. In fact, researchers believe that babies as young as six months have the ability to differentiate between a happy and an angry adult face. This is because we process these emotions in different areas of the brain. Smiles activate the left temporal area of the brain, while unhappy expressions activate the right temporal area. Research has also shown that our brains associate anger with masculinity. During a study, people were shown two androgynous faces; one with a smile and one with strained lips. Despite having no other facial characteristics, most people who participated in the study identified the smiling face as female and the angry face as male.

All the chemicals that go through your body when you're angry can have a physical toll on it. It has been shown that spending a lot of time angry can increase your risk of developing heart disease. It can also lead to a decline in lung function, as well as increasing physical aging of our bodies. As well as our physical health, being excessively angry is also not good for our mental health. Research has shown that it can worsen any anxiety problems one may have, as well as hinder their treatment.

But, it isn't all that bad; anger can also be a source of motivation. When your brain kicks into anger mode, it also activates the left hemisphere, the side of the brain usually activated by positive emotions. The positive aspects of anger can be trained back to our ancestors in the hunter-gatherer years. When they were angry, they were able to bargain more effectively, as well as co-operate more with each other. Anger can also often be linked with empathy, as people often become enraged about the suffering of others.

Signs of an Anger Disorder

While it is completely normal to experience anger every so often, someone with an anger disorder experiences anger outside of the normal emotional scope and have a great deal of difficulty controlling that anger. When diagnosing an anger disorder, a health professional will examine both physical and emotional symptoms.

Emotional Symptoms:

Failing to deal with anger can lead to a wide range of emotional states; these include irritability, rage, and anxiety. Having an anger disorder can also result in someone feeling overwhelmed, having trouble organizing their life, or fantasizing about causing harm to you or to others. Depression also can often come hand in hand with an anger disorder. The rage caused by an anger disorder can often lead to the sufferer lashing out. When this happens they will often feel guilty and alienate themselves as a result. When someone suffers with depression of a long period of time, it can be difficult for him or her to deal with his or her emotions. This increases the likelihood of an outburst, resulting in a vicious circle that is hard to break.

Physical Symptoms:

Strong feelings of anger can also cause physical changes in the body. Letting it go unaddressed of long periods of time can damage your overall health and but you at higher risk of ending up with a serious health problem. Physical symptoms of an anger disorder include:

- Tingling sensation
- Heart palpitations, increased heart rate, or a tightness in the chest
- An increase in blood pressure
- Headaches
- Tiredness or fatigue
- Pressure in the head or sinus cavities

Not addressing or diagnosing an anger disorder can have a long-term effect on both your physical and emotional health. Sufferers are at greater risk of having a stroke, can experience memory loss, have chronic sleep disorders, as well as great difficulties maintaining healthy relationships.

If you think you might have an anger disorder, you should speak to a professional such as a counsellor or a physician. You should never self-diagnosis or allow the results of a self-assessment test to choose your course of treatment.

Types of Anger

There is no definitive list of types of anger, with many researchers disagreeing, but the most widely accepted forms are as follows:

- Chronic Anger
- Passive Anger
- Overwhelmed Anger
- Self-inflicted Anger
- Judgemental Anger
- Volatile Anger
- Constructive Anger

Chronic Anger

Chronic anger is a type of anger condition, which results in sufferers becoming raged or ill tempered frequently. The sufferer is often upset easily, even over trivial matters. Many sufferers of chronic anger alienate their family and friends. Family and friends of a chronic anger sufferer can find it uncomfortable and at times even frightening to be around that person. Chronic anger usually develops gradually, usually over a period of years. It often begins in teenage or adolescence years.

Passive Anger

Passive anger is a type of anger that can be hard to identify. Those experiencing passive anger may, in many cases, not even realise that they are angry. It can come across in many forms including sarcasm or apathy. Passive anger may also result in someone behaving in a self-defeating manner. They might alienate themselves from their family and friends or decide to skip school or work frequently. They may also act awkwardly in social situations. Passive anger is often repressed and can be hard to recognize.

Overwhelmed Anger

This type of anger is usually caused by a particular situation. This situation is usually one that creates circumstances, which the sufferer finds difficult to deal with. This type of anger is also closely linked with frustration. Situations that can result in overwhelmed anger include a tight deadline, an overwhelming schedule, or struggling to raise children.

Self-Inflicted Anger

This type of anger is directed at the sufferer themselves as opposed to anyone or anything else. The sufferer sees him or herself as incompetent or a failure. This can result in either physical or emotion self harm. It could also manifest in ways such as an eating disorder or self-deprecation.

Judgemental Anger

This anger is caused when one makes an unfavourable judgement about a particular person or situation. It is in many ways a form of resentment or loathing. This type of anger manifests itself by the sufferer directing scathing or hurtful comments at the source of the anger.

Volatile Anger

Volatile anger is a type of anger that comes and goes, but when it comes it is intense. It is one of the more dangerous types of anger, often triggered by personal annoyance. It can cause explosive physical or verbal outbursts.

Constructive Anger

Constructive anger is a positive type of anger. It motivates people to make positive change, an example of which would be protesting. This type of anger demonstrates the survival value of our emotions.

It is important to remember that the list outlined above is not conclusive. Each person experience with anger will be different. It also important to realize that anger can fall into more than one of the mentioned categories. This list is only meant to be used as a rough guideline, if you feel like you have an anger disorder you should consult a professional, this list is for information purposes and should not be used for self-diagnosis.

How can Anger affect your Workplace/Relationships?

Frequent and excessive anger can have a devastating impact in the workplace environment. This is especially true in cases where anger manifests itself as violence. But even non-violent expressions of anger can be hindering. It cann cause employees to strike or riot. Some anger within the workplace might not even be expressed at all. Anger in the workplace can lead to hurt feelings, disruptive behaviours, and mental preoccupation. There are also personal effects, which include poor career prospects as well as poor health. Anger is bad for business; it results in a decrease in innovation, time wasting, increased employee turnover, and an increase in absenteeism.

It is a common misconception that venting anger is better than holding it in. Recent research has in fact shown that there are negative effects that come with venting your anger freely. Not looking after your physical and emotional health can damage your career. Chronic anger is especially damaging, and could result in long-term health problems.

The effect of the emotional components of anger in the workplace

- Diminished Caution
- Inability to reason
- Feeling of dominance
- Impulsiveness
- An increase in animation

The effect of the physical components of anger in the workplace

- Increase in heart rate
- Surges of Epinephrine
- Increase in blood pressure
- Tensing up of muscles
- Adrenaline rush
- Feeling clammy or sweaty

The potential problems that anger can cause in your career

- Co-workers hold a grudge against you
- You could become the possible target of a lawsuit

- A bad reputation for losing your temper easily
- You could become a target of revenge
- People will not want to talk to or work with you
- You will not be invited to participate in high-priority projects
- Vendors, clients, customers, and co-workers will want to avoid you

Long-term health problems caused by chronic anger

- Poor immune system
- Increased risk of Gastritis
- Increased risk of heart attack
- Increased risk of kidney disease
- Increased risk of stroke
- Frequent headache
- Increase in blood pressure
- Increased risk of suffering from a respiratory disorder
- Increased risk of arthritis
- Increased risk of a skin disorder
- Increased risk of a circulatory disorder
- Increased risk of a disability of the nervous system

Anger in the workplace affects both the company and the sufferer themselves. The company will suffer due to low commitment and efforts, which cause significant financial consequences as well as possible legal consequences. It also affects the people on the receiving end of the anger, the targets. They can experience sadness, fear, and thoughts of revenge.

Anger doesn't always start with a superior and works its way down the company, it can also work its way upward. Examples include attempts to undermine, failure to communicate, or failure to cooperate.

However, it's important to remember that anger, which is appropriately controlled, can actually be productive in the workplace.

How anger can improve productivity in the workplace

- It channels energy to fuel intensive work
- Results in perseverance

- Encourages innovation and creativity
- Encourages debate, which results in better outcomes
- Allows a company to identify what practices and policies are effective
- Motivates people to better competitors
- Motivates people to face wrongdoers
- Draws attention to an perceived injustices

Of course, anger is not solely focused on the workplace environment; relationships can also be a source of anger in our lives. Relationships, especially romantic relationships, are complicated at the best of times. We need to constantly work on them. Anger can be, and often is, a recurring theme in many relationships. Anger in relationships also often has deep roots and if left unaddressed can be destructive.

When it comes to anger in relationships, it is important to get to the root of what is causing it. Anger affects so many relationships because people usually hold on to the emotions of unresolved hurt and project them onto those closest to them. While you might view your anger as a form of protection, your partner will likely view it as destructive behaviour towards him or her. If you have feelings that have been repressed for an extensive period of time, it can be extremely difficult to talk about them. Couples counselling may prove effective for some couples, giving them a safe space to explore any repressed emotions. Being intimate with someone means showing him or her your vulnerabilities and accepting their vulnerabilities. While this is easy for some people, for others it results in aggressiveness and anger. Learning how to express your feelings and communicating with your partner will help your relationship greatly.

Chapter 2

Mistakes that fuel Anger

Common Situations that Trigger
Excessive Anger

Anger is our natural response to
perceived threats. It can be caused by
events that are both internal and
external. The following are common
situations that can trigger excessive
anger:

- Feeling threatened
- Coping with verbal or physical
  abuse
- A knock to our self-esteem or
  place within a social group
- Being interrupted or held back
  when trying to achieve a goal
- Losing out, especially when
  money is at stake
- Someone who is going against a
  principle which we consider to
  be important
- Feeling like we are being treated
  unfairly
- Feeling powerless

- Feeling disappointed in ourselves
- Feeling let down by those around us
- Having our property mistreated

Research has also shown that in some cases family background can play a role in how we express and deal with anger. In a high percentage of cases, people who came from disruptive and chaotic families, as well as families who were not skilled at discussing their emotions, were more likely to be easily angered.

Anger and Other Emotions

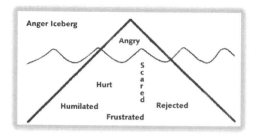

Anger is often described as a secondary emotion. What does this mean? It means that we often use anger as an emotion to cover up other feelings that we perceive makes us vulnerable. Therefore, the primary emotion would be how we feel before we become angry. This is illustrated in the diagram above. Fear, rejection, humiliation, frustration, pressure, and hurt are all examples of primary feelings that are often followed by anger.

Anger is similar to a lot of other emotions because many negative emotions, such as jealousy, loneliness, and sadness, can actually be translated into anger if they are intense enough. Anger doesn't just come all by itself; it is initiated by some other feeling.

Anger differs from emotions related to happiness because it is considered to be a negative emotion. It is not an emotion that could be maintained over a long period of time. There is nothing wrong with being happy everyday, but feeling angry everyday is not good. Anger is also usually an approach emotion, meaning it usually leads to some kind of action.

Anger and Self-Sabotaging

What is self-sabotage? It is when people, who are in a good position in their life, choose to engage in behaviour that is foolish. This behaviour includes killing themselves, hurting themselves, staying in an abusive relationship, cheating on their partner, speeding, stealing, refusing to eat, binge drinking, over eating, alienating themselves, or refusing to seek medical health when ill. Unconsciously, somewhere inside them is a death wish. Some people are more prone to this type of destructive behaviour than others.

Every child wants to be loved and accepted. Most children receive unconditional love from their parents. They are constantly reminded how loved they are. Unfortunately, this is the case for all children. Some are told that they are unwanted. That they are a nuisance and are not loved. Other vulnerable groups in society, such as members of the LGBT community, or African Americans, are also often looked down upon by other groups in society and constantly told they are different and not accepted.

Some parents, without even realising it, encourage their kids to self-sabotage. They refuse to teach their children coping skills, instead telling them that they will protect them. They refuse to teach their children skills to survive in what can be a hostile and frightening world. Without intending to, the parents are communicating to their children that they don't care whether or not they can cope in the world. They grow up with unrealistic views that the world revolves around them. Children who grow up with the view that they have either too much or too little power can misjudge situations easily and are likely to get hurt in the process.

If children are made to feel unwanted by their parents or by society, they begin to feel worthless. They begin to not value their existence and may develop an internalized death wish. This can be seen in statistics that show the younger death rate for African-American males, and the high suicide rates among LGBT youth. When children lack the skills to cope, they don't know how to deal with strangers, complicated situations, disappointments, abuse, or violations of their boundaries and privacy. They are far more likely to accidently find themselves in dangerous situations.

Often, those who are in minority groups in society, destroy themselves out of despair. Some African Americans die in gang feuds. Others drink themselves to death or turn to drugs as a coping mechanism. People who have been abused suffer even after the abuse has stopped; often they think the abuse was their own fault and that they deserved it, this results in them engaging in self-sabotaging behaviour. People who grew up in a home where they were made to feel worthless will often engage in self-sabotaging behaviour throughout their live. They see it as a way to maintain their shame, as a means to validate their worthlessness. This shame is almost always connected to addictive behaviour and suicide.

People who engage in self-sabotaging behaviour need to be re-parented. They need to surround themselves with people who will love, nurture, and validate them. They need to come to the realization that those who hurt them were in the wrong and that they are not worthless, quite the opposite. Healing from this internalized shame takes time. The sufferer needs to come to know that they are loved and that everybody is worthy. There are many different paths to healing one can take; examples include attending a support group, attending therapy, journaling and letter writing. Over time, sufferers will learn the skills needed to live a full live and thrive in it.

In most cases of self-sabotage, the person engaging in the self-sabotaging behaviour does not know how to vent their anger appropriately. They may be angry at the world or at whoever or whatever limited them. They might be angry about feeling like they are unworthy and unloved. They could be angry with the people around them who are loved. They might be angry with anyone around them who tries to love them or care about them. This anger is all part of the self-sabotaging behaviour. Sometimes it can be passive anger, hidden as depression, other times it can be expressed in violent behaviour and outbursts. Self-sabotage will usually manifest in some form of inappropriately expressed anger.

"Good Will Hunting" is a good example of a movie that illustrates the internalization of shame and self-hatred, and inappropriately expressed anger. It is a good example of self-sabotage and could be a useful tool in the healing process.

Self-sabotage is not uncommon; in fact, statistics indicate that 20% of people regularly engage in self-sabotaging behaviours. They also inappropriately vent their anger at themselves or those around them.

Anger and Family/Friendships

Anger within families is not at all uncommon. It can display itself in a wide variety of forms; examples include, domestic violence, child abuse, marital conflict, and sibling rivalry. As mention earlier, most people tend to direct their anger at the people closet to them, the people they love. Every family is complex, how each person acts within a family affects the other people in the family. Without drastic action, it is not possible to completely free yourself from the family. Members of a family often feel helpless to change the anger within it due to the complexity of family dynamics.

Generally, there are three different ways that anger can affect the family: it can be inherent, it can carry over from work or other stressful situations, or it can serve a specific function.

Some people are described by others as having a temper. A temperament is a person's customary manner of emotional response. Often times, a member of a family could be described as having a temper. They could be moody, intense, react badly to situations, and dislike any change in their life. This type of behaviour is biologically inherited; they react in a different manner to life's stressful events. You cannot completely alter someone's temperament, but it can be modified and better managed.

This is especially important for parents to understand. If they are having difficulty with a child they need to realise that it is not their fault, it is simply the child's temperament. It is also the reason why parents often have more difficulty with one child than another. When a parent has a completely different temperament to a child, it can be difficult for them to understand each other. In a similar manner, family members with the same temperament may rub each other the wrong way and will most likely engage in arguments far more frequently. There can often be power struggles between temperamental family members.

Displaced anger also frequently affects families. Displaced anger is anger that comes from one system to another. An example would be a family member who brings their work anger home with them. Having a bad day at work doesn't mean you should carry that frustration home with you and take them out on other members of your family. Your family are the people who love you unconditionally and stick by you no matter what, even if you get angry. This can't be said for everyone. If you get angry with your boss once too often he or she might fire you. If you frequently take your frustrations out on your family it can have negative consequences on your relationship. It can break down your ability to trust one another and feel safe with each other.

Anger is powerful. It has a specific social function. It signals to us that there is a problem, a need is not being fulfilled or there is a problem that needs to be solved. This can be seen is newborn babies, when there is something wrong they cry. If they do not get what they need they can become angry. This is seen by them shaking and screaming until their needs are met.

Anger can also be used as a means of control; this is often demonstrated by young children throwing a tantrum. The purpose of the tantrum is to get what they want. Tantrums are not limited to small children; teenagers and adults also have them. Anger can gain control in the short-term, but in the long-term it will break down relationships.

There are some simple tools that can be used to manage anger in the family. Firstly, it is important to take responsibility for your anger. You may not have control over the situation that made you angry, but you do have control over how you react and what you do with the anger. The blame game is the root of family destruction. There are no winners in the blame game, only losers.

The second tool is to find healthy ways to vent your anger; this could be an alternative outlet, such as sports, to release the pressures that build up throughout the day. Alternatively, if you feel like you are going to have an outburst you could leave the room or ask for some time alone. Meditation could also prove to be a helpful relaxation tip for many.

Thirdly, is becoming more aware of how we talk to ourselves. What do we say to ourselves in certain situations that cause us to react differently than other family members? Our emotions are influenced by self-talk.

Lastly, it is important to have a strong support network. It is important to have people to turn to in times of crisis. These people do not need to be family members, they could be friends, neighbours, or work colleagues.

Anger doesn't just affect families, it can also affect friendships and in some cases even and them. For a friendship to work both parties need to feel like they can be completely themselves, a bad temper can make this difficult. Easily is one party feels like they have to monitor what they say for fear of angering the other.

The more someone has verbal outbursts, the bigger the problem is. In the world be live in, technology can also often be used to express anger. It can be easy to type a rant that ends up scarring your relationship.

It is not uncommon for a bad tempered friend to engage in the following behaviours:

- Scream at you or cause a scene over something minor
- Let a calm discussion turn into a screaming match in a matter of seconds
- Stomp out or throw things when things aren't going their way
- Post a rant online calling out a friend who they feel has wronged them

If you are someone with a bad temper it is important that you:

- Apologize to a friend. If you have an outburst don't just ignore it and then wonder why your friend doesn't want to speak to you. Address issues as they arise to avoid build ups of emotion.

- Take care of yourself and keep your life balanced. Get enough sleep, eat healthy and exercise.
- If you are finding it to difficult to handle your temper yourself, seek professional help. They will help you get to the bottom of what is it that is causing these feelings and outbursts.
- Watch out for triggers that set you off. This will help you learn to cope and hopefully better control your outbursts. If things you read on social media set you off, then avoid those sites.

Trust in a friendship is harmed when one friend blows up at another, after all a friendship is supposed to be a safe space. One quick outburst can harm a friendship for years, especially if the issue is never properly addressed. A friend with a strong temper will make it difficult for their friends to confide in them. These friendships are also far more likely to end abruptly.

It might be easy for the person who lost their temper to move on as if nothing happened but their friends will not forget. If the situation is not discussed the negativity it caused will remain. The person who got angry might have gotten over it, but the other people involved might not have.

We all want to help our friends in any way we can, but sometimes we are not capable of providing the help they need. No matter what, we should never put ourselves in danger of getting abused, either physically or emotionally. If a friend has an outburst and is genuinely sorry about it, you can discuss it once the dust has settled. But if the outbursts are frequent, it'd be better to point them in the direction of professional help. Spend your time with someone who knows what a healthy friendship is about, someone who appreciates you.

Chapter 3

Anger Management Strategies

Cope with Anger, Or Cure It?

When dealt with appropriately, anger is a healthy human emotion; there is no cure for it. For someone who is suffering with an anger disorder there are some ways they can learn to cope with their anger and better control it.

As we have already examined, learning to control and cope with our anger is important for the following reasons:

- Out of control anger damages our physical health and wellbeing. We are not programmed to constantly operate at high stress levels. Sufferers of chronic anger are far more likely to have the following health problems; heart disease, diabetes, higher than normal cholesterol, weakened immune system, insomnia, and increased blood pressure.
- Out of control anger is not good for our mental health. When we

are constantly in a state of anger, it is much harder to concentrate or look at the bigger picture. Those who suffer with chronic anger are far more likely to suffer with depression or other mental health issues.

- Out of control anger hurts your career. While heated debate can at times be healthy as well as productive, lashing out inappropriately only serves to alienate yourself from your colleagues, and eventually you will lose their respect. A bad reputation in one job can also follow you around and stop you prospering in something else.
- Out of control anger hurts your relationship with those closest to you. Chronic anger makes it harder for people to feel comfortable with you, they may not feel like they can trust you or confide in you.

So, when learning to cope with our anger, where do we begin?

What is really behind your anger?

Why is your fuse so short? Your anger could be because of a traumatic event in your life or high levels of stress, it could even stem from your childhood. In most cases, anger is a cover-up for something else that we are feeling, you need to get behind your anger and deal with the underlying issues. Are you truly angry or is the anger masking under feelings that you are refusing to address.

So how do you know if you are truly angry or if there is more to your anger than meets the eye?

- You struggle to come to compromises. You find it difficult to understand other people's views. You might believe than compromising is a sign of failure or vulnerability. This is especially prominent in cases where someone grew up in a household where the angry person always got their way.
- You have trouble expressing any emotion apart from anger.
- You view other people's viewpoints as a personal challenge. You believe that you are always right and get angry

when anyone disagrees with you.
You see other people's opinion
as a challenge rather than another
perspective.

It's important to become comfortable
with every emotion instead of living
with one response to every situation. A
person who is unable to deal with the
full range of human emotions will live a
life of confusion, isolation, and self-
doubt.

The Dynamics of Anger

- When we are stressed we are far
  more likely to experience anger
- We are rarely angry for the
  reasons we think we are
- Anger can often come from not
  having our emotional needs met
  as a child
- Seeing a trait in others that we
  don't like about ourselves can
  often be a source of anger
- Disappointment is often a trigger
  of anger
- Experiencing abuse as a child
  can cause anger in a person
  throughout their adult lives

- Events that bring up unresolved issues from the past can be a source of anger

Be aware of your warning signs and triggers

When we are becoming angry, our bodies experience physical warning signs. Our bodies go into overdrive. The signs vary from person to person and it is important to learn what yours are. How does anger feel in your body?
- Stomach in knots
- Clenching your fists or jaw
- Becoming hot and flustered
- Increased heart rate or a pounding sensation in your chest
- Headaches or migraines
- Pacing or feeling restless
- Having trouble with your memory or concentration
- Tensing in your muscles, especially your shoulders and back

When someone has an anger disorder there anger is more related to the thoughts in their own head than the situations they believe are the cause. The following are common thought patterns that fuel anger:

- Overgeneralizing, for example, the belief that no one ever listens to what you have to say.
- Obsessing about the way you believe that things should be.
- Jumping to conclusions without fully hearing out what someone has to say.
- Looking for things to get upset about, while overlooking anything positive.
- Blaming someone else every time something goes wrong rather than taking responsibility for your own life.

If you choose to understand the people and situation that bring out the worst in you, you can avoid them.

Identify what it is in your day that is the source of these feeling and address it.

Think about ways that you can avoid the situation or it that's not possible, ways you can approach it differently.

Learn ways to cool down

Once you acknowledge what your warning signs are you can deal with your anger before it becomes uncontrollable. Here are some techniques you can put into practice:

- Focusing on the physical sensations anger causes can in many cases lessen the emotional intensity of it.
- Take deep, slow breaths.
- Take a brisk walk or play your favourite sport to release any built up energy.
- Listen to your favourite music or lie down and imagine you are in your favourite place.
- Massage any areas of your body that are feeling tense.
- Slowly count to ten in your head. Do so as many times as is necessary.

Remove yourself from the situation and ask yourself the following:

- Is this important in the grand scheme of things?
- Is it worth getting angry about?

- Is it worth affecting the rest of your day?
- Is your response appropriate?
- Is there anything you can do to make the situation better?
- Is taking action worth your time?

Find a healthy way to express your anger

When expressed in the right way, anger can be a tremendous source of inspiration for change. Firstly, you need to pinpoint what it is that you are actually angry about. By identifying the actually issue we will be in a better position to communicate our frustrations.

If the situation becomes too heated, remove yourself from it. Leave the room and take a few moments alone to cool down.

Realise that while it is important to express your needs, you also need to respect the needs of others. Winning an argument should not be a priority, not if it means breaking down a relationship. Don't bring up past situations, focus on the present. Don't spend time on petty conflicts that aren't worth your time or energy. Be willing to forgive, otherwise it will be impossible to resolve a conflict. If you are struggling to come to an agreement, know when to let go.

It isn't always possible to deal with our anger ourselves, in some cases it we may need to consider seeking professional help:

- You have tried everything but can't shake the constant feeling of frustration.
- Your temper is damaging your relationships both at work and at home.
- You have to avoid certain situations because of your temper.
- Your temper has gotten you in trouble with the law.
- Your anger has a tendency to lead to physical violence.

The following are tips for someone who's loved one is dealing with an anger disorder:

- Set out your boundaries, make it clear what you will refuse to tolerate.
- Talk about it when you are both calm, not when one of you is angry.
- If your loved one is having an outburst, remove yourself from the situation until they calm down.
- If you are struggling to stand up for yourself you might consider seeing a therapist.
- Never compromise your safety. If you feel threatened at any time, remove yourself from the situation and go somewhere that you know is safe.

Repressed Anger

It is important to learn how to express anger in a healthy way. Left unexpressed, it can be toxic. There are many instances where a person might feel that their anger is dangerous and that it is safer to hold it in. One example of such a person is a person who fears rejection. They can become empty, being whoever it is that those around them want them to be, afraid to be unloved. This is something that is often developed in childhood, especially if someone has grown up in a hostile home.

Repressed anger can affect us physically. It can be the cause of headaches, skin ailments, and heart problems. A person who represses his or her anger is likely to be someone who is very passive aggressive. Repressed anger is dangerous; holding in our frustrations can lead to a meltdown.

In order to let go of passive aggressiveness, we need to learn to, and not be afraid to, express our needs. By communicating how you feel, your anger is challenged in a healthy way and can be dealt with accordingly. If you are angry, you should be able to communicate this without losing your temper completely. The aim is to assert yourself with no aggression. You need to be able to communicate the following:

- How you feel
- What you want
- What you think

Usually, the fear of rejection is the underlying problem when it comes to repressed anger. This underlying fear is what holds a person bad from expressing themselves. Being able to express your needs is the goal.

Freeing yourself from repressed anger is important. Outlined below are some tips to help you identify the problem, and release the emotional pain, a handy tool to be able to put into use when necessary.

Repressed angry isn't healthy; you're pretending something doesn't exist when it does. You need to acknowledge the existence of anger. Anger itself doesn't cause a problem in our lives; it is how we choose to react to it. Here are some tips for coping with anger instead of ignoring it:

- Acknowledge its existence. Anger, like all emotions, comes and goes. Don't just ignore it.
- Don't push it away or reject it. Accept anger for exactly what it is, an emotion.
- Don't judge yourself for feeling angry, it's neither good nor bad, it's just a feeling.

- Let go of your anger, don't hold on to it. Thinking about what it is that made you angry over and over again will not help, in fact it will make you feel worse. If you find yourself obsessing, just take a moment, breathe in and say stop. Do something positive instead, something you enjoy, be it reading your favourite book or taking a walk.
- Remember that you are not your emotion. You are not your anger.
- Just because you are angry doesn't mean you have to act on it. Often, at the height of our anger we do something that we end up regretting. Get a grip on your anger before you react to it. You don't want to be beating yourself up further down the line over something you did or something you should have done.
- Don't repress your anger, accept it.

For the following exercise you will simply need a pen, paper, and some alone time. Make sure you are comfortable and in an environment you feel completely safe in. The purpose of the following steps is to help you identify the areas of your life where anger is a problem and then address why this is the case.

Step 1: What happened?
This simply involves jotting down the details of a situation that left you feeling hurt, unappreciated, betrayed, ignored etc. Be prepared for the fact that you might have to explore hurtful memories that you have been ignoring to date.

Step 2: Who was involved?
Who was involved in the situation and in what way? Spend some time on this step; really explore what it was that this person did to make you feel bad. Was it intentional? Or did they just say or do the wrong thing without even realising they had hurt you?

Step 3: What are your opinions?
Look at what you have written about the person or people involved. You obviously have opinions about them and they are most likely not favourable. This is your chance to write down exactly what your opinions are of them. This is especially therapeutic if you are someone who usually lives by the

phrase, "if you can't say something nice, don't say anything at all". Take 2 minutes to let all the ugliness inside of you out, free your mind.

Step 4: What did it cost you?

What did you lose in the situation? Or what did the situation stop you doing? Did you have to give up something important to you? Remember that not everything is black and white. You might actually discover that there were positives that came from the situation.

Step 5: Take out any built up aggression

If you have repressed anger, you likely didn't attack the person who caused you to feel this way. The energy and rage is mostly still likely built up within you. It's time to let it out. Grab something soft, like a pillow or large cuddly toy, and attack. Punch it repeatedly; you will be surprised how good it feels to release all the built up frustration.

Step 6: Time for self-care

It is likely that you are also angry with yourself for whatever role you played in the situation. It's time to let go of all the blame. You need to step a lot of time on this important step. Concentrate on feelings of comfort, love, and compassion. Forgive yourself. This step is all about you, your health, and your peace of mind.

Step 7: Create new agreements
Look over everything you have written so far. Think about how you could handle this situation better in the future. What part did you play and what lessons have you learnt?

This step is all about being proactive and taking responsibility for your own life. It's time to be the most powerful version of you possible. You have the power to change any aspect of your life at any moment. Stop and no, are just some of the words you have at your disposal. Create a new set of terms concerning how you will deal with similar situations in the future.

Set yourself boundaries, physical and emotional. These are agreements that you are making with yourself; they do not concern anybody else. Now live in accordance to the new agreements you have made.

Strategies for Self-Relaxation

*"If a man insisted always on being
serious, and never allowed himself a bit
of fun and relaxation, he would go mad
or become unstable without knowing it".*
Herodotus

Modern live is full of stress, and this
stress is often a source of anger in our
lives. If you find that the stresses of your
daily life are bringing you down, it could
be beneficial for you to learn some
simple relaxation techniques. Relaxation
is all about controlling our state of mind.
There is no point going for a massage in
order to relax if the whole time you are
going to be thinking of nothing only a
bad situation that happened at work.

When it comes to relaxation, here and
now is all that matters. You will never
be able to fully relax if you are always
worrying about the future or the past.
Worrying about something serves no
valuable purpose. We can't change the
past and we certainly can't predict the
future. To live in the moment is to live in
a state of relaxation.

Our environment plays an important role in relaxation. You probably notice that you find it far easier to relax in some rooms than in others. Being surrounded by clutter can hold so back from relaxing fully, it can be a constant source of reminding about things that we have to do and can weigh a heavy burden on our mind. By simply tidying up our room we can make a big change and create an environment to relax fully in. Spend some time making your space as enjoyable as possible; invest in your favourite flowers or a candle in your favourite scent. Get some fluffy blankets and make a pile of your favourite books or cds. Feeling relaxed will result in a more productive you. Relax. You deserve it and it is good for you, plus it takes less time than you may think.

You do not need a spa weekend or a retreat to relax. Here are some stress and anger busting tips to help you relax in less than 15 minutes:

Meditation
It only takes a few minutes of meditation a day to help greatly reduce anxiety, stress, and anger levels in your life. Research has suggested that just five

minutes of meditation a day has the ability to alter the neutral pathways in your brain. This then makes you more resilient when it comes to coping with stressful situations. Meditation is not at all difficult, it is in fact one of the quickest and simplest things you can do to relax. Pick the most relaxing room in your house, or perhaps the garden if it is a nice day. Sit up straight and place both of your feet on the floor, make sure you are completely comfortable and shut your eyes. Allow no negative thoughts to cross your mind, repeat a positive mantra, such as "I am happy" or "I love myself" over and over in your head. Put one hand on your belly and breathe deeply, time and sync your breaths in time with the positive words in your mind.

Inhale Deeply
You only need five or ten minutes to completely a relaxing breathing exercise. All it involves is taking a break to think about and focus on nothing only your breathing. Sit yourself in a position similar to the one described above for the meditation exercise. Put your hand on your belly; breathe in through your nose, deeply and slowly. When your

lungs are full, exhale slowly through your mouth. Breathing deeply slows your heart rate and lowers your blood pressure, it has the exact opposite effects to stress and anger making it a great counteractive exercise.

Live In The Moment

We have a tendency to rush through our day, never really taking notice of anything or appreciating all that we have. It's important to take some time in your day to remember to slow down. Life isn't a race. For five minutes, focus all of your attention on just one thing. It could be anything; how the wind feels against your face, the sound of rain hitting the window pane, the taste of your meal. You will find that when you focus completely on one moment, your stress and anger will begin to fade.

Reach out to those around you

The best tools for handling stress and anger are often those closest to you, your family and friends. Take time in your day to chat to them, preferably face to face. Share your worries and goals and take time to ask about theirs in return.

Pay Attention to Your Body

When you are having a stressful day, concentrate on how it is making your body feel. Either lie down on your back or sit up with your feet on the floor. Move each part of your body, starting at your toes, and pay attention to how each part of your body feels. This exercise isn't about changing anything; it's just about noticing where in your body is tensed up, it's all about giving your body some attention.

Decompression

For ten minutes, sit or lie in a relaxing position and pack a warn heat pack on any tense areas of your body. Anger usually causes tenseness in your shoulders and back so it might be useful to concentrate on these areas. Close your eyes while the heat pack gets to work. Make sure all your muscles are fully relaxed. After ten minutes have passed, remove the heat pack. Use a foam roller or a handheld massager to massage your muscles and remove any remaining tension. Alternatively you could ask your partner or a close friend to massage your muscles for you. Whatever you are most comfortable with.

Laugh Out Loud

A good laugh does absolute wonders for your health, as well as lightening your mood. It lowers the level of cortisol in your body, a stress hormone released when you are stressed. It also raises the levels of endorphins in your body, a hormone with the opposite effect to cortisol, instantly lifting your mood.

Listen to your Favourite Music

Listening to music can have a great affect on your mood. Its soothing effects actually work to reduce your heart rate, blood pressure, and stress levels. Put together a playlist of your favourite music, it could be anything from the current hits to the sounds of nature. Whatever you choose, focus on nothing only what you're hearing and allow it to soothe your soul. You can also let go of any anger by rocking out to some rock music or singing along slowly to your favourite band. Music therapy is a recognized way of improving mental health.

Exercise

Exercise releases endorphins. It doesn't have to be high intensity exercise either, even the simplest of movements work.

Not everyone is built to be a runner. Even some slow and simple yoga poses or a slow walk and can a stress busting effect on the body. Exercise gives your body a healthy outlet for any frustration whilst releasing feel good chemicals. Exercise is a great help for sufferers of depression. It helps us become calm and relaxed, and also helps us to sleep better at night. Regular exercise will also have an effect on our physical body, boosting our confidence. If you are struggling to know where do begin you can always ask your family doctor to give you an exercise programme suited to you.

Be Grateful
When we are always concentrating on the negative, it can be easy to forget the positive. Keeping a gratitude journal can help you begin to notice and appreciate all the good in your life. Being thankful and appreciative will help combat any negative thoughts you might have. You can start by writing out all the things you are thankful for that have happened in your life to date, and then you can write a daily entry at the end of each day acknowledging everything good that happened. You should also use it to acknowledge things that you

accomplished and are proud of, no matter how insignificant it might seem. When you are having a tough day, look through what you have written in your journals to remind yourself that it isn't all that bad.

Mindfulness
Mindfulness is a trendy word at the minute, and is being thrown around a lot, but what exactly does it mean? Mindfulness could be described as meditation's sister; they are quite similar in many ways. Mindfulness involves appreciating something in the present moment whilst blocking everything else out. It could be something as simple as appreciating the sounds or colours of nature whilst out of a stroll. You can practice mindfulness in as little as two or three minutes. Try focusing all your thoughts and energy on a mundane everyday object. To have the ability to be able to focus all your thoughts and energy on something in the present moment, that is the essence of mindfulness.

Try some Yoga
Yoga is a great tool for relaxation and it calms the mind as well as relaxes the

body. You do not have to spend an hour attempting complex poses to reap the benefits. There are some little poses anyone can do that are just as effective. Here is a simple pose to practice; lie on your back with your legs bent, place your feet flat on the floor, place your hands on your belly and watch them rise and fall with your breath. Let your shoulders be heavy, push them towards the ground. Just two or three minutes in this pose can have a great calming effect. If you have practiced yoga before, you can try some more complex poses. Backbends are particularly excellent. They are a great cortisol buster. If you are a yoga beginner, ease yourself into things; trying complex poses with no practice can do more harm than good. A yoga class could be beneficial for beginners; the guidance of a professional will ensure you avoid injury.

Have a cup of Tea
It may be a cliché, but a nice cup of tea can help, if not solve, many problems. Chamomile tea is especially favoured in times of stress for its properties, which have a calming effect on the mind. However, even regular black tea has been shown to reduce cortisol levels.

Go outside

If you are feeling frustrated, stressed, overwhelmed, or angry, taking a few minutes break and stepping outside could make the world of difference. Breathing in some fresh air will help to clear your head and give you a new perspective on whatever it is that is bothering you. Spending just 20 minutes a day outside can be beneficial for both our physical and mental health.

This list is in no way exhaustive, different relaxation strategies work for different people. What works for you may not work for someone else. Some people might find that reading a book or a magazine is the best way for them to relax. Others might find gardening or even cleaning the house to be therapeutic. Discover what it is that works for you. Spending as little as 15 minutes doing something that you love can make the world of difference in your mood. You could have sex, watch your favourite television show, walk the dog or play with the cat. We all get angry and stressed from time to time in life, so it is important to have ways that you can deal with them.

Conclusion

Anger doesn't always have to be negative, if managed and expressed in a healthy way it can play a positive role in our life. If you find you are having difficulty controlling your temper, and it is having a negative impact on your life, getting to the root of your anger is the most important step. Once you fully understand what it is that is causing your anger, you will be in a better position to understand and address it. Don't be afraid to reach out to those around you and ask for help if you need it, we don't have to face anything alone, which is one of the joys of being human.

"Anybody can become angry — that is easy, but to be angry with the right person and to the right degree and at the right time and for the right purpose, and in the right way — that is not within everybody's power and is not easy."
— Aristotle

Did You Enjoy This Book?

I want to thank you for purchasing and reading this book. I really hope you got a lot out of it.

Can I ask a quick favour though?

If you enjoyed this book I would really appreciate it if you could leave me a positive review on Amazon.

I love getting feedback from my customers and reviews on Amazon really do make a difference. I read all my reviews and would really appreciate your thoughts.

Thanks so much.